Sunrise Book

All Times Children's Stories

Selection from the Panchtantra

Preface

Welcome to the wonderful world of imagination - of magic, of adventure, of animals that speak, of happenings that are strange and marvellous! This is a series of five books, carefully graded with regard to language and concept. The stories have been adapted from a wide variety of sources - the Panchatantra, Aesop's Fables, the Brothers Grimm, Hans Christian Anderson and folk tales from all over the world. Colourful illustrations bring alive the characters.

We hope that through these books, children will discover the matchless pleasure of reading and will embark on a fascinating journey of discovery and delight.

Contents

SUNRISE PUBLISHERS

32/33A, Street No. 9, Bhikam Singh Colony, Vishwas Nagar, Shahdara, Delhi - 110032 (India)

Tel : +91-11-71218130, Whatsapp No. : +91-7835078000

E-mail : sunrisepub@gmail.com, export@sunrisepublisher.com

Visit us : www.sunrisepublisher.com

ISBN : 978-81-781304-8-4

Printed by **Tan Prints (India) Pvt. Ltd.**, Village Rohad, Distt. Jhajjar, Haryana

1. The Talking Cave

One day a lion was looking for food. However, he could not find a single animal.

`What shall I do?' thought the lion.

Just then he came to a cave. 'I'm sure some animal lives here,' said the lion to himself. 'I'll hide inside the cave and when the animal comes in, I'll eat him up.'

So he hid inside the cave. Now a jackal lived in that cave. When he came home he stopped in surprise. He could see the footprints of some animal going into the cave. He could see none coming out.

`I'm sure a lion or a tiger is hiding inside,' thought the clever jackal. 'As soon as I go in, he'll eat me up.'

Then he had an idea. He said, 'Cave! My dear friend! Why haven't you welcomed me?'

The lion was very surprised. Did the cave really speak? Did it really welcome the jackal home everyday?

`Dear cave!' said the jackal again. 'Why don't you speak to me? Is someone hiding there? Are you trying to warn me? Shouldn't I come in?'

Now the lion thought that the cave must really be calling out to the jackal. He thought the cave must really be welcoming home the jackal everyday. So he said, 'Welcome, friend! Welcome home!'

The jackal gave a shout of laughter. So a lion was hiding in the cave!

I've seen a lots of caves,' said the clever jackal, 'but I've never seen one that talks!' Then he ran away.

2. The Four Wise Men

Once there were four young men. They had spent many years studying. One day their teacher said, Now you know all that I could teach you. Go out into the world. Use what you have learnt wisely.'

So they set out. They came to a forest. There they saw the bones of a lion.

`Let's see how much we know,' said one of them. 'Let's bring this lion to life.'

`What a good idea!' said the others.

`Well, I can put the bones together,' said the first wise man.

`I can give it flesh, blood and skin,' said the second.

`And I', said the third, 'can bring it to life.'

`And I think you shouldn't do that,' said the fourth wise man.

But the other three did not listen. The first wise man put the bones together. The second gave it flesh, blood and skin.

Now I'm going to put life into it,' said the third wise man.

`Wait! Wait!' shouted their friend. He quickly climbed a tree. He watched as his friend put life into the lion.

The lion gave a loud roar as it came to life. The three wise men smiled at each other.

`How wise we are!' they said.

But the next moment their smiles changed to screams of fear as the lion jumped on them. It soon tore them to pieces.

Ah well,' said the fourth wise man. 'You must really use your learning wisely.'

3. The Clever Hare

Once there lived a big lion. Everyday he used to chase and kill animals. The animals were very worried. They held a meeting.

`What shall we do?' they asked each other.

`I know what we'll do,' said a fox. 'Let's draw lots and send one animal to the lion everyday. Then he can stop killing so many animals each day.'

`What a good idea!' said the others.

So the animals went to the lion and told him their plan. The lion was very pleased. He agreed at once.

So everyday the animals sent one animal to the lion. One day it was the hare's turn. As he walked on slowly he thought, 'How can I get rid of the lion?'

Just then he saw a well. He could see his reflection in it. He now had an idea.

He went to the lion and said, 'I'm sorry, I'm late but there's another lion in the jungle. He wanted to eat me. When I told him about you, he said he was the King of the Jungle.'

'He said that!' said the lion angrilly.

`Yes, he did,' said the hare. 'And he wanted to fight you.'

'Is that so?' shouted the lion. 'Take me to him. I'll fight him! I'll show him who the King of the Jungle is!'

So the hare took him to the well. 'He's in there,' said the hare. 'I'm afraid of him. You go on ahead.'

The lion peeped in. He saw his reflection. He gave a loud roar. The roar echoed back from the well. The lion thought that it was another lion.

`I'm going to fight you!' he shouted. He jumped in and was drowned.

The clever hare ran back happily. How pleased the other animals were!

`What a clever hare you are!' they cried. 'You've saved our lives!'

4. The Farmer And The Three Thieves

Once there was a farmer. One day he bought a fat goat from the market. He began to walk home with the goat on his shoulders. His way lay through a forest. Three thieves saw him.

`Let's get the goat from the farmer,' said one. 'Yes, then we'll have a good dinner,' said the second. 'I have a plan,' said the third. He told his friends his plan and they all hid themselves.

As the farmer walked by, the first thief came out in front of him. 'Good evening,' he said. 'Why are you carrying your dog on your shoulders?'

'Dog?' cried the farmer. Are you blind? I am carrying a goat."Oh, well,' said the first thief. 'If you say it's a goat, it's a goat. Who am I to disagree?' Then he walked away.

Now after a while, who should the farmer meet but the second thief. 'Good evening,' he said. 'Is your dog sick? Is that why you are carrying him?' Dog?' cried the farmer. 'Are you blind? I am carrying a goat.'

`Well,' said the second thief. 'If you want to call a dog a goat, you can.'

Then he, too, walked away.

The farmer was very surprised. What was wrong with everybody? Or was it really a dog that he was carrying? He took down the goat and had a good look. Of course, it was not a dog. It was a goat.

`There must really be something wrong with the eyes of the two men I met,' he said to himself. He put the goat on his shoulders and walked on. He was now at the edge of the forest and only a short distance away from home.

Now he met the third thief. The third thief stood in the middle of the path and began to laugh. He laughed so much that tears ran down his cheeks.

The farmer was very surprised. He could see nothing funny. He stopped and said, 'Why are you laughing?'

`Well,' said the third crook. 'You look so funny carrying that dog on your shoulders! I've never seen a funnier sight in all my life!' Then he began laughing again.

The farmer gave a cry of fear. He dropped the goat and ran home as fast as he could. 'Thank God, I'm safe,' he said to his wife. 'It was not a goat that I had bought but an evil spirit that kept changing its shape.'

And what happened to the goat? The thief caught it and killed it. Then he and his friends roasted it over a fire and had a very fine dinner!

5. The Iron Balance

Once there was a trader's son called Veera. He had lost all his money so he decided to go to another town and try his luck. He had an iron balance which his father had given him. He went to his father's friend who was also a trader and said, 'Uncle, I am going to another town. Will you please keep my iron balance safe for me until I come back?'

The trader said, 'Of course I will.'

So Veera left his iron balance with his father's friend and went to the next town. When he came back after several months he went to the trader and said, 'Uncle, please give back my iron balance.'

The trader did not want to return it. So he said, 'Son, I cannot do that because rats have eaten it.'

Veera said, 'Don't worry, Uncle. Such things happen. Now I am going to the river to have a bath. Please send your son, Deva, with me to look after my things.'

So the trader sent his son, Deva, with Veera. Veera went to the river and

hid Deva in a cave. Then he came back to the trader.

`Where's my son?' asked the trader.

`A big bird came and carried him off,' said Veera

`A big bird!' cried the trader. 'You liar! How can a bird carry off a young man?'

`Well,' said Veera. 'If rats can eat an iron balance, a bird can carry off a young man!'

The trader turned pale.

`Forgive me, my son,' he said. 'I have been greedy. I have made a mistake.'

He returned Veera's iron balance and Veera returned Deva to him.

6. The Monkey And The Crocodile

Once there was a monkey. He lived in a mango tree beside a river. He was very friendly with a crocodile that lived in the river. Whenever the crocodile came out, the monkey would give him mangoes to eat and to take home.

One day Mrs. Crocodile said to Mr. Crocodile, 'Where do you get this sweet fruit from?'

Mr. Crocodile said, 'My friend, the monkey, who lives in the mango tree, gives it to me.'

Mrs. Crocodile said, 'Bring him to me. I want to eat his heart. He eats sweet fruit so his heart must be sweet too.' The crocodile said, `I'm never going to let you eat my friend's heart.'

But Mrs. Crocodile said, 'I want his heart!' again and again - morning, noon and night. Finally the crocodile got sick and tired of hearing her say the same thing again and again.

So he went to the monkey and said, 'You're invited for dinner to my house. Climb on my back and I'll take you.'

So the monkey climbed on his back. When they reached the middle of the river, the crocodile said, 'I have a surprise for you. I'm not taking you for dinner. You are our dinner!'

`Me?' cried the monkey in surprise. 'Why me?'

`Well,' said the crocodile. 'Mrs. Crocodile wants to eat your heart.'

`Is that all?' said the clever monkey. 'Then why didn't you say so before? I always leave my heart hanging from the mango tree for safety. Let's go back and I'll give it to you.

So the crocodile took him back. As soon as they got to the shore, the monkey jumped off the crocodile's back. He quickly climbed his mango tree. Then he said to the crocodile, 'You foolish creature! Don't you know that a person's heart is inside his body? How can someone leave his heart behind? Now get lost! I can never again be friendly with a wicked fellow like you!'

7. The Turtle And The Cranes

Once a turtle and two cranes lived beside a lake in a forest. They were the best of friends. They ate the fish in the lake, they drank the cool clear water and lived there happily. The happy days, however, did not last long. One year there was no rain. The lake began to dry up. All the fish and water plants began to die.

`It's time for us to leave the forest,' said one crane to the other. 'Yes,' said the second crane. 'We must find another place to live in.'

Take me with you!' shouted the turtle. Take you?' repeated the cranes. 'But how? You can't fly.'

`Well, you can carry me,' said the turtle, quite pleased that he would soon be travelling by air!

`Oh no!' said the cranes. `You're too heavy.' They sat down and together tried to work out a plan. Suddenly the turtle gave a great shout of joy. `I know what!' he shouted. `I know what! Go and get a big, strong stick. Then you two can hold each end of it in your beaks and I'll hold the middle of the stick with my teeth and then .....' `And then, we'll fly!' cried the cranes. `You clever, clever turtle! What a wonderful idea!'

So one of the cranes flew quickly and returned with a long, strong stick. `Let's get ready for the flight,' said the first crane. 'But you must not talk on the way.' You'll see and hear a number of things,' said the second crane. `But don't open your mouth.' Of course, I won't,' said the turtle. `I know I'll fall if I do.'

So the two cranes took the two ends of the stick in their beaks and the turtle caught the middle with his strong teeth and off they flew! What a wonderful sight they made as they flew in the sky - two cranes and a turtle on a stick! At first the turtle was afraid and shut his eyes tight. But when he opened his eyes - what beautiful sights he saw! Never had the turtle seen anything like it - hills, valleys, lakes lay spread out before him like a giant map. He was about to say so when he remembered in time. He did not open his mouth.

They now passed a field, where farmers were harvesting grain. `Oh look!' cried one of them. 'Look at those clever cranes! See how they're carrying their friend! What a good idea!'

The turtle thought this was quite unfair. After all it was HIS idea. He ought to have been called clever. The turtle quite forgot what he had been told. He shouted, `It was MY idea!'

But the moment he opened his mouth, he fell. Down, down, down he went. Where did he land? Nobody knows.

'I do wish he had listened to us,' said the cranes sadly.

8. The Greedy Brother

Once there was a farmer. He had four sons. They were very poor. Often there was nothing to eat in the house. One day he said to his sons, 'You must go out into the world. See if you can earn money. Come back when you're rich.'

So the four young men set out to earn some money. They soon came to the edge of a forest. There they saw a very old man. 'Don't worry, my children,' he said. 'Let me help you.' He gave each of them a cotton wick.

`Wherever a wick falls,' he said, 'you must dig. You'll find something. Take it and return home.'

So the four brothers thanked the old man and walked on. As they came to a stream, the first brother dropped his wick. He stopped and began to dig. He found a jar full of copper coins. He was very happy and said to his brothers, 'Let us take this and go home.'

But his brothers did not want the copper coins. So he said good-bye to his brothers and went home. His brothers walked on. Soon the second brother dropped his wick. When he began to dig he found a jar of silver coins. He was very happy. He said to his brothers, 'Let us take this and go home.'

But his brothers did not want the silver coins. So he said good-bye to his brothers and went home. His brothers walked on. Soon the third brother dropped his wick. He began to dig. He found a jar of gold coins. 'How wonderful!' he cried. 'Now we'll all be rich. Let's go home.'

But the fourth brother said, 'The first brother found copper coins, the second brother found silver coins and you've found gold coins. Maybe, I'll find jewels.'

The third brother said, 'Don't be greedy. Let's go home.'

But the fourth brother said goodbye to his brother and walked on.

Now he came to a forest. There he saw a young man. His body was covered with mud. On his head was a wheel that kept going round and round.

The fourth brother was very surprised. He walked up to the young man and said, 'Why are you sitting here? Why is there a wheel on your head?'

The moment he asked this he found himself sitting on the ground with the mud on his body and the wheel on his head. The man who had been sitting there, got up.

'I, too, was greedy like you,' he said. 'So I was punished. Now you must sit there with the mud on your body and the wheel on your head until another greedy person comes along and asks you why you are sitting here.'

9. The Jackal King

Once a jackal was hunting for food. He fell into a pot of indigo dye. When he came out - he was bright blue in colour.

The animals were very frightened when they saw him. `Who is this creature?' cried some. 'We've never seen such an amazing thing in all our lives!' cried the others.

The jackal was very pleased. 'Everyone is afraid of me,' he said to himself. 'No one knows that I'm a jackal.'

So he said, 'I'm the Great Indigo Ruler! I am your new king!'

The animals were so frightened of him that they made him their king at once. Everyday all the animals, even the lion and tiger bowed low before him. The animals brought him the best fruits they could find. The jackal was very pleased. He chased away the other jackals. He said to himself, 'A great king like me doesn't need these stupid jackals.'

How the other animals feared the jackal! How the jackal enjoyed himself!

One night, after dinner, when the jackal was nearly asleep he heard some jackals howling. The jackal was very pleased.. It was a long time since he had heard a jackal howl. He quite forgot that he was the Great Indigo Ruler. He howled back in reply.

At once the lion and tiger recognised him. 'This Great Indigo Ruler is only a jackal!' they cried. 'How foolish we have been!'

Then they pounced on the jackal and killed him.

10. The Crow And The Snake

Once there lived two crows in a big tree. In the hollow of that tree lived a big black snake. Now whenever Mother Crow laid her eggs the snake would come out of the hollow and eat her eggs.

`Oh dear!' cried Mother Crow. 'What am I to do? This wicked snake eats up all my eggs. How can I bring up my babies?' Don't worry,' said Father Crow. 'I'll speak to him.'

So Father Crow went to the snake. He said, 'Please Sir, don't eat up our eggs. I'll find frogs for you to eat. If you eat up our eggs how can we bring up our babies?' The snake hissed. 'I don't care about your babies,' he said. 'I love eggs and you can't stop me from eating them.'

Poor Father Crow sat sadly on a branch. 'What am I to do?' he said. 'What will I tell Mother Crow?' A jackal who had been watching said, 'Father Crow, do as I say. Go to a rich man's house. Pick up a gold necklace. Make sure everyone sees you. Then bring it to your tree and drop it in the hollow.'

So Father Crow flew to the big, beautiful house of a rich man. He found that the rich man's wife was just going in for a bath. He saw her take off her gold necklace and keep it on a table in the courtyard. He cawed loudly. As soon as the servants came out, Father Crow picked up the necklace and off he flew. He was chased at once by angry servants. Father Crow came to his tree and dropped the necklace in the hollow of the tree. Then he flew up to a branch and sat down to wait.

The servants came running up to the hollow. To their surprise they found that a big, black snake was coiled up inside. 'A snake!' they cried. 'Quick - bring out your sticks! Kill it! Kill it!'

So they brought out their sticks and killed the snake. Then they picked up the necklace and went back.

What about Father Crow? He was very pleased. He thanked the jackal and went home to tell Mother Crow the whole story. So Mother Crow and Father Crow had lots of babies and lived happily ever after.

11. The Four Friends

Once upon a time a stag, a crow, a turtle and a mouse became friends. They all lived together happily in a big forest.

One day the stag was caught in a hunter's net. 'Oh dear!' he cried. 'What shall I do?'

When the stag did not return at lunch-time, his friends began looking for him. The crow flew all around the forest. At last he saw his friend. He flew down to the stag at once.

`Dear friend,' said the crow, 'Don't worry. I'll save you.' Then he flew back. He brought the mouse who quickly bit through the hunter's net. Meanwhile the turtle, too, reached there.

`Dear friends,' said the stag. 'Thanks to you, I am free. Now let us get away quickly. The hunter will be here any moment.'

No sooner had he said this that the hunter came back. Away ran the stag! Away ran the mouse! And away flew the crow! But the turtle was not able to get away quickly. Quick as a wink, the hunter caught him.

`If I don't have a stag, at least I'll have a turtle to eat!' he said. So he tied up the turtle, put him on his shoulder and began to walk away.

The animals were very upset. They didn't know what to do. At last the crow said, 'I have a plan!' He told his plan to his friends and they all followed the hunter. The crow saw the path he was taking and the three friends went ahead by a short-cut.

Hardly had the hunter gone a little further when he saw a stag lying in his path. A crow was sitting on his head pecking at his eyes.

`Ah!' cried the hunter. 'This is the stag that had got away. I think that it is dead because that crow is pecking at his eyes. Now I'll have the stag and the turtle too!'

So he dropped the turtle and rushed to the stag. As soon as his back was turned, the mouse went up to the turtle and bit through his ropes. And quickly the two of them hid in the bushes.

When the hunter reached the stag, the crow cawed loudly and flew away. The stag shook his huge head and jumped to its feet. Then he too ran away!

The hunter was very surprised.

'How strange!' he said to himself. 'Well, at least I have the turtle!'

But when he turned back - what a shock he got! There was no turtle there. Sadly, he went back.

As for the four friends - they danced with joy !